This recipe book b

Recipe Index

	No.		No.
	1		26
	2		27
	3		28
	4		29
	5		30
	6		31
	7		32
	8		33
	9		34
	10		35
	11		36
	12		37
	13		38
	14		39
	15		40
	16		41
	17		42
	18		43
	19		44
	20		45
	21		46
	22		47
	23		48
	24		49
	25		50

Recipe Index

	51		76
	52		77
	53		78
	54		79
	55		80
	56		81
	57		82
	58		83
	59		84
	60		85
	61		86
	62		87
	63		88
	64		89
	65		90
	66		91
	67		92
	68		93
	69		94
	70		95
	71		96
	72		97
	73		98
	74		99
	75		100

RECIPE NAME

SERVES

PREP TIME

TIME TO COOK

NOTES

INGREDIENTS

DIRECTIONS

RECIPE NAME

INGREDIENTS

SERVES

PREP TIME

DIRECTIONS

TIME TO COOK

NOTES

RECIPE NAME

SERVES

PREP TIME

TIME TO COOK

NOTES

INGREDIENTS

DIRECTIONS

RECIPE NAME

SERVES

PREP TIME

TIME TO COOK

NOTES

INGREDIENTS

DIRECTIONS

RECIPE NAME

SERVES

PREP TIME

TIME TO COOK

NOTES

INGREDIENTS

DIRECTIONS

RECIPE NAME

SERVES

PREP TIME

TIME TO COOK

NOTES

INGREDIENTS

DIRECTIONS

RECIPE NAME

SERVES

PREP TIME

TIME TO COOK

NOTES

INGREDIENTS

DIRECTIONS

RECIPE NAME

INGREDIENTS

SERVES

PREP TIME

DIRECTIONS

TIME TO COOK

NOTES

RECIPE NAME

SERVES

PREP TIME

TIME TO COOK

NOTES

INGREDIENTS

DIRECTIONS

RECIPE NAME

SERVES

PREP TIME

TIME TO COOK

NOTES

INGREDIENTS

DIRECTIONS

RECIPE NAME

SERVES

PREP TIME

TIME TO COOK

NOTES

INGREDIENTS

DIRECTIONS

RECIPE NAME

SERVES

PREP TIME

TIME TO COOK

NOTES

INGREDIENTS

DIRECTIONS

RECIPE NAME

SERVES

PREP TIME

TIME TO COOK

NOTES

INGREDIENTS

DIRECTIONS

RECIPE NAME

INGREDIENTS

SERVES

PREP TIME

DIRECTIONS

TIME TO COOK

NOTES

RECIPE NAME

SERVES

PREP TIME

TIME TO COOK

NOTES

INGREDIENTS

DIRECTIONS

RECIPE NAME

INGREDIENTS

SERVES

PREP TIME

DIRECTIONS

TIME TO COOK

NOTES

RECIPE NAME

SERVES

PREP TIME

TIME TO COOK

NOTES

INGREDIENTS

DIRECTIONS

RECIPE NAME

SERVES

PREP TIME

TIME TO COOK

NOTES

INGREDIENTS

DIRECTIONS

RECIPE NAME

SERVES

PREP TIME

TIME TO COOK

NOTES

INGREDIENTS

DIRECTIONS

RECIPE NAME

SERVES

PREP TIME

TIME TO COOK

NOTES

INGREDIENTS

DIRECTIONS

RECIPE NAME

SERVES

PREP TIME

TIME TO COOK

NOTES

INGREDIENTS

DIRECTIONS

RECIPE NAME

SERVES

PREP TIME

TIME TO COOK

NOTES

INGREDIENTS

DIRECTIONS

RECIPE NAME

SERVES

PREP TIME

TIME TO COOK

NOTES

INGREDIENTS

DIRECTIONS

RECIPE NAME

SERVES

PREP TIME

TIME TO COOK

NOTES

INGREDIENTS

DIRECTIONS

RECIPE NAME

SERVES

PREP TIME

TIME TO COOK

NOTES

INGREDIENTS

DIRECTIONS

RECIPE NAME

SERVES

PREP TIME

TIME TO COOK

NOTES

INGREDIENTS

DIRECTIONS

RECIPE NAME

SERVES

PREP TIME

TIME TO COOK

NOTES

INGREDIENTS

DIRECTIONS

RECIPE NAME

SERVES

PREP TIME

TIME TO COOK

NOTES

INGREDIENTS

DIRECTIONS

RECIPE NAME

INGREDIENTS

SERVES

PREP TIME

DIRECTIONS

TIME TO COOK

NOTES

RECIPE NAME

INGREDIENTS

SERVES

PREP TIME

DIRECTIONS

TIME TO COOK

NOTES

RECIPE NAME

INGREDIENTS

SERVES

PREP TIME

DIRECTIONS

TIME TO COOK

NOTES

RECIPE NAME

SERVES

PREP TIME

TIME TO COOK

NOTES

INGREDIENTS

DIRECTIONS

RECIPE NAME

SERVES

PREP TIME

TIME TO COOK

NOTES

INGREDIENTS

DIRECTIONS

RECIPE NAME

SERVES

PREP TIME

TIME TO COOK

NOTES

INGREDIENTS

DIRECTIONS

RECIPE NAME

SERVES

PREP TIME

TIME TO COOK

NOTES

INGREDIENTS

DIRECTIONS

RECIPE NAME

SERVES

PREP TIME

TIME TO COOK

NOTES

INGREDIENTS

DIRECTIONS

RECIPE NAME

SERVES

PREP TIME

TIME TO COOK

NOTES

INGREDIENTS

DIRECTIONS

RECIPE NAME

INGREDIENTS

SERVES

PREP TIME

DIRECTIONS

TIME TO COOK

NOTES

RECIPE NAME

SERVES

PREP TIME

TIME TO COOK

NOTES

INGREDIENTS

DIRECTIONS

RECIPE NAME

INGREDIENTS

SERVES

PREP TIME

DIRECTIONS

TIME TO COOK

NOTES

RECIPE NAME

SERVES

PREP TIME

TIME TO COOK

NOTES

INGREDIENTS

DIRECTIONS

RECIPE NAME

SERVES

PREP TIME

TIME TO COOK

NOTES

INGREDIENTS

DIRECTIONS

RECIPE NAME

SERVES

PREP TIME

TIME TO COOK

NOTES

INGREDIENTS

DIRECTIONS

RECIPE NAME

SERVES

PREP TIME

TIME TO COOK

NOTES

INGREDIENTS

DIRECTIONS

RECIPE NAME

SERVES

PREP TIME

TIME TO COOK

NOTES

INGREDIENTS

DIRECTIONS

RECIPE NAME

SERVES

PREP TIME

TIME TO COOK

NOTES

INGREDIENTS

DIRECTIONS

RECIPE NAME

SERVES

PREP TIME

TIME TO COOK

NOTES

INGREDIENTS

DIRECTIONS

RECIPE NAME

INGREDIENTS

SERVES

PREP TIME

DIRECTIONS

TIME TO COOK

NOTES

RECIPE NAME

SERVES

PREP TIME

TIME TO COOK

NOTES

INGREDIENTS

DIRECTIONS

RECIPE NAME

SERVES

PREP TIME

TIME TO COOK

NOTES

INGREDIENTS

DIRECTIONS

RECIPE NAME

INGREDIENTS

SERVES

PREP TIME

DIRECTIONS

TIME TO COOK

NOTES

RECIPE NAME

SERVES

PREP TIME

TIME TO COOK

NOTES

INGREDIENTS

DIRECTIONS

RECIPE NAME

SERVES

PREP TIME

TIME TO COOK

NOTES

INGREDIENTS

DIRECTIONS

RECIPE NAME

SERVES

PREP TIME

TIME TO COOK

NOTES

INGREDIENTS

DIRECTIONS

RECIPE NAME

SERVES

PREP TIME

TIME TO COOK

NOTES

INGREDIENTS

DIRECTIONS

RECIPE NAME

SERVES

PREP TIME

TIME TO COOK

NOTES

INGREDIENTS

DIRECTIONS

RECIPE NAME

SERVES

PREP TIME

TIME TO COOK

NOTES

INGREDIENTS

DIRECTIONS

RECIPE NAME

SERVES

PREP TIME

TIME TO COOK

NOTES

INGREDIENTS

DIRECTIONS

RECIPE NAME

INGREDIENTS

SERVES

PREP TIME

DIRECTIONS

TIME TO COOK

NOTES

RECIPE NAME

SERVES

PREP TIME

TIME TO COOK

NOTES

INGREDIENTS

DIRECTIONS

RECIPE NAME

INGREDIENTS

SERVES

PREP TIME

DIRECTIONS

TIME TO COOK

NOTES

RECIPE NAME

SERVES

PREP TIME

TIME TO COOK

NOTES

INGREDIENTS

DIRECTIONS

RECIPE NAME

INGREDIENTS

SERVES

PREP TIME

DIRECTIONS

TIME TO COOK

NOTES

RECIPE NAME

SERVES

PREP TIME

TIME TO COOK

NOTES

INGREDIENTS

DIRECTIONS

RECIPE NAME

SERVES

PREP TIME

TIME TO COOK

NOTES

INGREDIENTS

DIRECTIONS

RECIPE NAME

SERVES

PREP TIME

TIME TO COOK

NOTES

INGREDIENTS

DIRECTIONS

RECIPE NAME

SERVES

PREP TIME

TIME TO COOK

NOTES

INGREDIENTS

DIRECTIONS

RECIPE NAME

SERVES

PREP TIME

TIME TO COOK

NOTES

INGREDIENTS

DIRECTIONS

RECIPE NAME

INGREDIENTS

SERVES

PREP TIME

DIRECTIONS

TIME TO COOK

NOTES

RECIPE NAME

SERVES

PREP TIME

TIME TO COOK

NOTES

INGREDIENTS

DIRECTIONS

RECIPE NAME

INGREDIENTS

SERVES

PREP TIME

DIRECTIONS

TIME TO COOK

NOTES

RECIPE NAME

SERVES

PREP TIME

TIME TO COOK

NOTES

INGREDIENTS

DIRECTIONS

RECIPE NAME

| INGREDIENTS |

SERVES

PREP TIME

| DIRECTIONS |

TIME TO COOK

NOTES

RECIPE NAME

SERVES

PREP TIME

TIME TO COOK

NOTES

INGREDIENTS

DIRECTIONS

RECIPE NAME

INGREDIENTS

SERVES

PREP TIME

DIRECTIONS

TIME TO COOK

NOTES

RECIPE NAME

SERVES

PREP TIME

TIME TO COOK

NOTES

INGREDIENTS

DIRECTIONS

RECIPE NAME

SERVES

PREP TIME

TIME TO COOK

NOTES

INGREDIENTS

DIRECTIONS

RECIPE NAME

SERVES

PREP TIME

TIME TO COOK

NOTES

INGREDIENTS

DIRECTIONS

RECIPE NAME

INGREDIENTS

SERVES

PREP TIME

DIRECTIONS

TIME TO COOK

NOTES

RECIPE NAME

SERVES

PREP TIME

TIME TO COOK

NOTES

INGREDIENTS

DIRECTIONS

RECIPE NAME

SERVES

PREP TIME

TIME TO COOK

NOTES

INGREDIENTS

DIRECTIONS

RECIPE NAME

SERVES

PREP TIME

TIME TO COOK

NOTES

INGREDIENTS

DIRECTIONS

RECIPE NAME

INGREDIENTS

SERVES

PREP TIME

DIRECTIONS

TIME TO COOK

NOTES

RECIPE NAME

SERVES

PREP TIME

TIME TO COOK

NOTES

INGREDIENTS

DIRECTIONS

RECIPE NAME

INGREDIENTS

SERVES

PREP TIME

DIRECTIONS

TIME TO COOK

NOTES

RECIPE NAME

SERVES

PREP TIME

TIME TO COOK

NOTES

INGREDIENTS

DIRECTIONS

RECIPE NAME

INGREDIENTS

SERVES

PREP TIME

DIRECTIONS

TIME TO COOK

NOTES

RECIPE NAME

SERVES

PREP TIME

TIME TO COOK

NOTES

INGREDIENTS

DIRECTIONS

RECIPE NAME

INGREDIENTS

SERVES

PREP TIME

DIRECTIONS

TIME TO COOK

NOTES

RECIPE NAME

SERVES

PREP TIME

TIME TO COOK

NOTES

INGREDIENTS

DIRECTIONS

RECIPE NAME

INGREDIENTS

SERVES

PREP TIME

DIRECTIONS

TIME TO COOK

NOTES

RECIPE NAME

SERVES

PREP TIME

TIME TO COOK

NOTES

INGREDIENTS

DIRECTIONS

RECIPE NAME

INGREDIENTS

SERVES

PREP TIME

DIRECTIONS

TIME TO COOK

NOTES

RECIPE NAME

SERVES

PREP TIME

TIME TO COOK

NOTES

INGREDIENTS

DIRECTIONS

RECIPE NAME

INGREDIENTS

SERVES

PREP TIME

DIRECTIONS

TIME TO COOK

NOTES

RECIPE NAME

SERVES

PREP TIME

TIME TO COOK

NOTES

INGREDIENTS

DIRECTIONS

RECIPE NAME

INGREDIENTS

SERVES

PREP TIME

DIRECTIONS

TIME TO COOK

NOTES

RECIPE NAME

SERVES

PREP TIME

TIME TO COOK

NOTES

INGREDIENTS

DIRECTIONS

RECIPE NAME

INGREDIENTS

SERVES

PREP TIME

DIRECTIONS

TIME TO COOK

NOTES

RECIPE NAME

SERVES

PREP TIME

TIME TO COOK

NOTES

INGREDIENTS

DIRECTIONS

Made in the USA
Columbia, SC
10 May 2019